A Modern Guide to Renting in 2019

A step-by-step roadmap for finding, leasing, and moving into your ideal rental

Copyright © 2018 by Elizabeth Peek

Icons created by Andrejs Kirma from the Noun Project

All rights reserved. No part of this book may be reproduced in any form without the permission in writing from the author. Reviewers may quote brief passages in reviews.

No part of this publication may be reproduced or transmitted in any form or by any means, mechanical or electronic, including photocopying or recording, or by any information storage and retrieval system, or transmitted by email without permission in writing from the publisher.

Disclaimer and FTC Notice

While all attempts have been made to verify the information provided in this publication, neither the author nor the publisher assumes any responsibility for errors, omissions, or contrary interpretations of the subject matter herein.

This book is for entertainment purposes only. The views expressed are those of the author alone, and should not be taken as expert instruction or commands. The reader is responsible for his or her own actions.

Adherence to all applicable law and regulations, including international, federal, state and local governing professional licensing, business practices, advertising, and all other aspects of doing business in the US, Canada, or any other jurisdiction is the sole responsibility of the purchaser or reader.

Neither the author nor the publisher assumes any responsibility or liability whatsoever on the behalf of the purchaser or reader of these materials. Any perceived slight of any individual or organization is purely unintentional.

Description

So you have made the decision to move out on your own. CONGRATULATIONS! Every move is exhilarating, nerve wracking, and totally free-ing. It provides the perfect backdrop to starting a new chapter in your life -- a new you. You can redefine yourself and shape your life into whatever you want. So let's make this your best move ever! *A Modern Guide to Renting* is your cheat sheet to finding, leasing, and moving into your ideal rental. You'll get contemporary information packed with helpful insights, handy worksheets, and tons of pro tips and tricks to save you big headaches and needless expenses.

Acknowledgements & Thanks!

Special acknowledgements to my parents, Lizette and Eduardo Cueto. For allowing me to be free and encouraging me to explore the world around me.

Thanks to my awesome husband, Garrett Peek, for encouraging me to put pen to paper; and helping me sort what is in my head.

Thanks to my Puerto Rican brother from another mother, Vinnie Romero, you rock! <boop>

CONTENTS

1. INTRODUCTION

2. PLANNING
    a. Setting Expectations
    b. Budgeting 1.0
    c. Understanding Credit Basics

3. GO TIME
    a. Apartment Hunting
    b. Budgeting 2.0
    c. Applying for a Lease
    d. Signing a Lease

4. FOLLOW THROUGH
    a. Budgeting 3.0
    b. Packing
    c. Before Moving In
    d. Moving Day

5. GETTING SETTLED
    a. Unpacking
    b. Utilities
    c. Address Change
    d. Legal Documents
    e. New Neighborhood

6. CONCLUSION

7. APPENDIX

INTRODUCTION

By way of introduction, my name is Liz. The first time I moved out of my parents' house I was 20 years old and I moved in with a friend who I had meet on a study abroad program the previous year. I have moved many, many, many times since then (15 times, across 8 cities, 3 states, 2 countries, and 2 continents to be exact).

By the time I was settled in New York City I made moving people around NYC my business. I was a Realtor for Citi Habitat, the largest apartment rental agency in NYC at the time. When I moved to Kansas with my family I continued my work in Real Estate and also got into investment properties in Kansas and in Florida and managing renters of my own.

My goal with this book is to help those in a position to move out maneuver the modern moving process and prepare for moving day, and beyond. However, every situation is unique and only you can make the decision on what is right for you. I can only offer advice based on my expertise.

That said, every move is exhilarating, nerve wracking, and totally free-ing. Moving provides the perfect backdrop to starting a new chapter in your life -- a new you. You can redefine yourself and shape your life into whatever you want. And if you put together a solid plan you are setting yourself up for success, not just for this move but for every other move you make throughout your life.

> "Planning is bringing the future into the present so that you can do something about it now."
> ~Alan Lakin, personal time management expert

PLANNING

So you have made the decision to move out on your own. CONGRATULATIONS! Perhaps you have gotten an acceptance letter, or you got a kickass job offer, or have decided that it is just time to go. Whatever your reasons are you should know that your family and friends may have reasons for you to stay. Rather than packing your bags and walking out the door "like a thief in the night" (my mother's words to me), perhaps you would consider taking a few minutes to layout your plan for those who care.

This act will give your family and friends peace of mind in knowing that you have thought this through and are making an informed decision -- as an adult. Open up the process to them, listen to their concerns and feedback. If they understand where this decision is coming from it is easier to get them on board. Besides, there are a lot of preparations to be made, goodbyes to be said, and packing to be done and you can <u>ALWAYS</u> use help on moving day!

> "The journey of a thousand miles begins with one step."
> ~ Lao Tzo

For the purposes of this book, I am going to assume that you know what city you are moving to. I am also assuming that you have visited the area -- at least once, or are going to soon. This sets you up to start with the end in mind. It helps to think of this adventure as a maze: your starting point is your current living situation and your end point is you living in your own place. Now you just have to sort through all the middle parts and hit all the checkpoints along the way. The maze itself is made up of how you handle the smaller tasks: research, questions, decisions, preparations, and challenges.

Apartment hunting can feel like a daunting task that lasts forever. But the reality is that this process can take a long as you need it to or you can go through this entire process in about one month (4-weeks) from start to finish. You should know, however, that in larger cities like New York, apartment hunting moves at lightning speed. There is such a high demand for apartments that there is no guarantee that the one you like will still be available when you are ready to move on it. Hence, do all your planning and legwork ahead of time so that when time comes to view apartments you will be ready to jump when you find the one you want.

Setting Expectations

Let me start by saying that the image of independence that you have in your head at this moment in time is most likely totally unrealistic. But it is a great place to start. Thinking about your new hypothetical living space, what kind of amenities (apartment attributes) are you looking for, there are no wrong answers; just go with it. Now write it all down.

I have included a worksheet in the appendix for you. Below are some example of each sections. Grab a pen, and let's get to work.

Step 1: List out all the amenities you want in your new space. Some popular amenities include:
- Air conditioner
- Bedrooms/rooms required
- In-unit washer & dryer (private units inside your apartment)
- In-building laundry facilities (public units shared with other apartment residence)
- Allows pets
- Dishwasher
- Some utilities included
- Balcony
- Cable ready
- Garage or covered parking
- Swimming pool
- Business center (printer access)
- Fitness center
- Gated access

- Walk-in closets
- Designated office space
- Close to downtown (bars, restaurants, nightlife, work)
- Access to public transportation
- Concierge service or doorman

AMENITIES WANTED

Air conditioner	Balcony
1 Bedroom	Cable ready
In-building public laundry	Elevator
Dishwasher	Close to public transportation
Some utilities included	Close to bars, restaurants, nightlife

Step 2: Ask yourself a few questions to understand your expected lifestyle.
Is there anything in my life that I just cannot live without?
Gym, restaurants, grocery stores, parks, public transit, library

What will a typical day be like for me?
Will you be working 8-5 Monday - Friday? Will you be in class 3 days a week?

Should I take my family pet with me or leave them home?

KEY QUESTIONS

Is there anything in my life that I just cannot live without?

Gym, restaurants, grocery stores, parks, public transit, library

What will a typical day be like for me?

Working 8-5 Monday - Friday. Class 3 days a week 6-9.

Should I take my family pet with me or leave them home?

No, leave Fluffernutter home.

Step 3: Categorize all of your amenities into "Must-Haves" and "Nice-to-Haves".

What are the amenities that you absolutely need and cannot live without, categorize these as must-haves. Perhaps just the fact that you have a separate bedroom (1-bedroom) from the rest of the living space is a must (vs. a studio apartment where all living spaces are combined into one main room).

Are there some amenities that you would consider nice-to-haves like having a washer/dryer inside your apartment? Meaning it would be great if it were inside your unit but not a deal breaker if it were down the hall.

By categorizing all the items on your list you are gaining clarity on what is important to you. Your categorized list will be a living document in that it will change constantly. Consider how it will change once you review it under a financial lens.

MUST-HAVE	NICE-TO-HAVE
Air conditioner	Balcony
1 Bedroom	Cable ready
In-building public laundry	Walk-in closets
Dishwasher	Some utilities included
Close to bars, restaurants, nightlife	Close to public transportation

Step 4: Reality check…*How are you going to be paying for it all?* Will you be working? Scholarships? Family allowances?

Understanding how you are going to afford living on your own will shift and morph this document to be more realistic. For example, once you have sorted out your budget you may find that some of the amenities in your must-have category suddenly fall to the nice-to-have category or vice versa. Sadly, each feature listed above has a price tag associated with it. Meaning money that you either have or don't. Take a look at the financial impact for just a few of the example amenities:

> Living in a solo apartment will cost more than living with a roommate, which will cost more than living in a dorm.
>
> Living in an area of town that is close to the action - bars, restaurants and activities is going to be more expensive than living in an area that is more rural with grocery stores and parks.
>
> If you are not planning to be home very often, perhaps you could get by with a cheaper studio apartment vs. the 2-bedroom apartment you might want if you plan to work from home.

A lot of apartment buildings charge a monthly "Pet Rent" in addition to a "Pet Deposit". <Cha-Ching!>

As you tour neighborhoods and apartments there may be some additional amenities that you add to your list that you had not thought of previously. And, do not be disappointed if your new living arrangements are not exactly as you envisioned at the start of this exercise. This is actually a good thing; your tastes are being refined and honed into what you really want.

Budgeting 1.0

Please do not treat the word "Budget" like a 4-letter word. It is not (obviously, it has more than 4-letters)! Having a budget is absolutely necessary and helpful. It is also something that everyone will be interested in. "What is your budget?" will be the first question from your parents, all the landlords and leasing offices, and your rental realtors (if you use one - totally not necessary).

A budget is just an itemized list comparing your EXPECTED income vs. your EXPECTED expenses/financial commitments over the same time frame. Ideally, budgets are done on a monthly basis but if you are on a fixed scholarship you may have to consider doing a budget per semester in addition to a secondary, more detailed monthly budget.

If you need help getting a personal budget started I highly recommend using Microsoft Excel and finding pre-formatted templates. You can also download templates from Pinterest (my favorite option). Budget templates will include basic line items along with blank lines so that you can include individual expenses that you may have. Below are a few examples of expected expenses to include:

- Rent: housing rent, parking space, storage units
- Utilities: electricity, gas, water, cable, and internet

- Insurances: renting insurance, car insurance
- Meals: supermarkets, restaurants/take-out, drive-thrus, delivery apps (e.g. Caviar or Postmates)
- Transportation: car payments, gas/tolls, vehicle registration, cabs/Uber/Lyft, flights, public transportation tickets/passes (e.g. bus, train, subway, light rail)
- Medical: prescription medication, over-the-counter medicine, co-pays
- Entertainment: date nights, impromptu adventures, vacations, movies (including Red Box and OnDemand rentals), concerts, spending cash
- Clothing and toiletries: new threads, laundry/dry cleaning budget, shoe repair, toiletries
- Subscriptions and memberships: gym, magazines, online movie or music services, box subscriptions, prepared food subscriptions
- Gifts: birthdays, weddings, baby showers and holidays
- Pet Care: food, toys, litter, annual checkups, flea medicine

When planning out your budget, do not max yourself out. Meaning if your take home pay is $1,500 per month, you will need to cover all your expenses and try to put some money away in case of a "rainy day". A rainy day could look like: a flat tire, a parking ticket, a late fee, or an extra doctor's bill. While this may be harder when you first move out, it is not impossible. Do not underestimate the power of saving $25 a month!

Working with a budget will help make the apartment hunting process feel real. It will clearly outline what you can afford and it will focus your search to realistic parameters. That said, your biggest expense in your budget will be your rent. Your ideal rent is approximately one-third of your monthly take-home income (after taxes). This is how it would look:

If your expected take-home income (after taxes) is

> $2,000/$**month** *you should be able to afford 33% for rent; or $660.*

When you are applying for an apartment the landlord will review your expected income and compare it to the asking rent. This is a form of risk assessment, the larger that percentage is, the riskier the tenant and the higher the chances the landlord may ask for a guarantor. More information is provided about a guarantor in the next chapter.

Once you have your rent range set you should re-evaluate your must-haves and nice-to-haves list. An apartment that has everything is not likely to fall into your budget. Which brings me to an old Spanish proverb - loosely translated:

> *Good, Pretty, and Cheap...never the 3 shall meet (Bueno, Bonito y Barato)*

Implying that a modern apartment complex with a pool, gym, all utilities included located in the middle of an up and coming new area is likely not going to be cheap.

There are two obvious routes that you can take to keep rent to a manageable amount: roommates and subleasing. Using the income example above, if you only have a max of $660 to spend on rent, you should consider having shared expenses. Finding roommates gives you the upper hand, especially if you are the incoming roommate. It is your choice if you finally decide to move into "that" space with "those" people.

Subleasing may be a great option if you are trying to get a feel for an unfamiliar area. With a sublease, the original lessee will usually leave their belongings in the apartment. Meaning that you will not have to purchase kitchen supplies or even bring your furniture. However, you will have to be respectful since you are borrowing someone else's things. A sublease can be for any amount of time: one week or even one year. However, you will want to make sure that subletting is allowed within the original lease.

Pet vs No Pet

Should you take your family pets with you when you move out? Or should you leave them at home with the rest of the family? This should be given considerable thought. Your schedule will be a major factor in this decision. If you are not planning to be home, due to work or school or both your pet will be home alone -- a lot. Which can lead to behavioral problems that may cause your pet to act out; e.g. eating your shoes or peeing on your bed.

You will also need to consider the financial obligations of owning a pet. You will need to buy food, toys, and treats for your pet and budget for vet visits. The average cost of owning a dog is approximately $1,300 a year. The average cost of owning a cat is approximately $1,100 per year. This does not include any major issues or vet care that would be needed.

And lastly, many apartments also have breed restrictions and/or weight restrictions. A majority of landlords charge "pet deposit" and a monthly "pet rent" to deter tenants from owning pets. If your new place has either of these, you will need to account for it in your monthly budget and moving expenses.

Understanding Credit Basics

No budget conversation would be complete without a section on Credit. Your credit score is probably the second most important number in the modern world, right behind your social security number. Credit does not just refer to a credit card, but rather your FICO score. I highly recommend that you go online and request a FULL credit report early on in your planning process. A full report will include your entire credit history from all three credit reporting bureaus: Equifax, Experian, and TransUnion.

Reviewing your report line by line in imperative. When you apply for an apartment your credit report will be pulled as part of your background check.

So make sure that everything seems correct. Meaning, all inquiries are legitimate, all balances are up to date, and that everything in the report IS, in fact, yours. If you find incorrect information in your report begin the process of correcting it or removing it ASAP. Incorrect information or even identity theft is a substantial problem and takes time to correct.

GO TIME

Armed with your budget, your credit score, an idea of what you want in your apartment and, you have enlisted your family to help on moving day...You are now ready to do the leg work to signing on the dotted line.

This stage will feel like you are creating an endless to-do list, but really you are creating an action plan. With an action plan you have sequential steps and a timeline. The steps in an action plan will also likely fit into categories that will flow into one another like a waterfall. These categories are: Apartment Hunting, Lease Prep, and Budgeting (2.0). The appendix has worksheets to help you flow right through this process. You will have a lot of work to do so keep a pen handy.

Apartment Hunting

To me, apartment hunting is the fun part. I know that some people may disagree, but everyone can agree that you have to do it. **Under no circumstances should you rent an apartment "sight unseen"**. Apartment hunting is your chance to see what is available. You get to walk through model apartments and envision yourself living in all these different spaces. You will likely see some great apartments and some dumpy ones. But you will not know which is which until you have actually walked through them.

PRO TIP

Do NOT give your social security number or money to anyone until you have walked through the actual apartment. There are a lot of scams with "landlords" asking for money to hold the apartment for you and the apartments do not actually exist.

Apartment hunting is hard work. When you start your search you will cast your net wide. There are a lot of places that you can search to find available apartments: the local newspaper, Craigslist, Facebook, apartment apps, and roommate apps. Below is an outline for how to sift through all the apartments to get to the one that is right for you.

Step 1) "Soft search." Look for ad placements and listings either online or in local papers. Grab any listing that looks interesting and review the ads carefully. The more listings you see the better you will be at deciphering listing language; e.g. "cozy" = small, "historic" = old.

Step 2) Take your list and drop each address into Google Maps. Get an idea of where the listing is located. Is this area right for you? How close/far is it from work or school?

Step 3) Call/text for info and schedule a time to view. Before you reach out, re-review the remaining posts some may fall off your list at this point too. Call, text or email the landlords and leasing offices that have placed the ads and try to find out as much information as you can before actually going to see the apartment. This will save you a lot of time later when you are scheduling to view the apartments.

When you call, do not worry if you do not know what to ask. *"Is it still available"* and *"What can you tell me about this apartment?"* are great opening lines. Usually, the person on the other side will be able to fill in the gaps. The more phone calls you make the more information you will gather, and the better questions you will think to ask.

Step 4) When you are ready to view apartments walk, bike, or drive around the neighborhood to get to know the area a bit. Also, take this opportunity to look for other "For Rent" signs and call them too. If you see a large apartment complexes that appeals to you, go in. Most large complexes have a leasing office that you can stop in and talk to someone about availabilities on the spot. Some may even have model apartments for you to check out.

I highly recommend that you keep track of each apartment using an apartment hunting checklist. I have included a sample apartment checklist in the appendix. Make a copy of it and keep it with you when you are viewing potential spaces. This will help to compare all the front running apartments on the same merits when the time comes.

> Here are a few **PRO TIPS** for things to consider when you are walking through an apartment for the first time:
>
> **Do not go apartment viewing alone.** Always go with another person. This is both for safety and to have an extra set of eyes on the space. While you are noticing the shiny new kitchen, your partner may notice that the bedroom window faces a brick wall.
>
> **Take a measuring tape** with you when looking at new places. This way you can ensure that your furniture will fit.
>
> **Visit potential apartments at night.** What is the area like? Does it still feel safe? Will there be plenty of parking in the evening? Is there enough street lighting?
>
> **Go apartment viewing in the day.** The shade of night covers too many imperfections. Lighting may not be great, and in some cases the power may be turned off.
>
> **Take pictures of each apartment** -- even the ones you do not like. After the first three they will all start to melt and morph together and you will be hard pressed to remember which apartment had what amenity.
>
> **Test the water pressure** in the shower and kitchen sink; individually and running at the same time.
>
> **Look inside everything:** the cupboards, closets, and cabinets. "For what?" you may ask...mice holes, rodent droppings, fleas, ticks and bedbugs (they don't just live in beds). No need to move into a place with existing tenants. If you have your sights set on

> this particular apartment, insist that the landlord address the issue BEFORE you move in.
>
> **Call your car insurance company** and run your potentially new address by them. This is especially important in up-and-coming areas. You may be surprised to find out that your car insurance rate could increase.

Step 5) Once you have seen several apartments gather your pictures and checklists; compare them to each other and then stack them against your must-haves and nice-to-haves list and, most importantly, to your budget. Especially consider the location of each. And not just the address, but the neighborhood around it. Are you close to a gym, restaurants, grocery stores, parks or public transit? Consider your commute on an extra hot summer's day or snowy winter's morning.

Budget Beware: Some apartments may include some or even all utilities into the rent. If they do not, you will be responsible for water, gas, and/or electric. This could have a big effect on your budget. Below is a list of common utilities that may or may not be included with your rent:

- Water
- Wastewater
- Gas
- Electricity
- Cable/Internet
- Phone
- Trash pickup
- Snow removal
- Parking

Budgeting 2.0

Before you request a lease application, take a moment to redo your budget. Replace your placeholder budget totals with the real rent and the average of the utility invoices. If you are responsible for utilities, you can call the utility companies and ask them for the _average invoice for the last 12-months_ for your specific apartment. If you are moving in with roommates, they will be able to provide you with average utility expenses.

What does your budget look like now? Can you still afford this apartment? Perhaps, you may have to rework some of you allowances. Or, perhaps the apartment building offers a gym, so now you do not have to pay for a membership! My point is - now that you have picked an apartment, your budget should be much more concrete and less hypothetical.

Applying for a Lease

Congratulations, you found your apartment! Time to request the lease application. Before you do this, you should know a few things. A landlord has every right to choose who they want to let rent their property. This means that they have the right to ask to see some personal information, like: your bank statements, previous tax filings, a credit report, a background check, and even reference letters. Most landlords these days are also checking out your social media profiles. I am not advising to change who you are on social media, but perhaps consider not posting any drunken shenanigans for a month before or after just to be safe.

When you are given the lease application, read through it carefully. You will likely have to provide some support materials and an application fee with the completed application. Landlords have the right to conduct background checks and if they do, you will have to pay for it and it is a non-refundable fee. This means that if you do not get the apartment (for whatever reason), you do not get your money back.

The information in the background check that landlords are receiving is:

Rental History: How long you have lived at each location and past evictions.

If you are moving out for the first time you will not have a rental history.

Work History: How long you have been working with each employer.

If you are moving to take a new job, you will be required to produce a letter from your new employer that states the position you are taking, the start date, and financial compensation.

Criminal History: Do you have a police record?

Credit History: Specifically, that you have paid your debts on time and that you do not chronically have late payments on your reports.

Guarantor

If you do not a have substantial credit history or if you have never rented an apartment before, the landlord may request a Guarantor. This is someone who can guarantee that you will not skip-out on your rent. Meaning, if you do not pay your rent, the landlord can legally require the Guarantor to pay it on your behalf.

If you need a Guarantor, they will have to fill out an application of their own and cover the cost for their own background check.

Signing a Lease

The lease application process will usually only take a day or two. Once you have been approved, you will be on your way to signing your lease. The lease is a legally binding document that outlines the stipulations of your rental agreement. Since this is a legally binding document, I highly recommend that you read it BEFORE you sign. Feel free to ask your new landlord to provide you with a copy of the lease ahead of time so that you can read it over before you both sign it.

The fact that this is a legal document should not scare you. Yes, it will likely be a few pages and will look official but, it is basically a rule book. Read it, understand it, and ask questions if you are not clear. You need to know what is expected of you before you move into your new place. In order to familiarize yourself with a lease I have provided a sample residential lease in the appendix. This is the lease that I have my tenants sign when I rent out my properties. Review it and you will see that it is nothing to be intimidated by.

The terms of your rental will be spelled out in the lease. Some examples include: terms for terminating the lease, pet policy, subletting restrictions, if you can have a barbecue, if you can have visitors who stay for more than a week, if you are required to have rental insurance, and even if you need to provide notification prior to having a party. These are all real limitations that I have personally seen in leases.

Your lease will also contain fee information and utilities information. Make sure that the utilities covered in the lease match what was advertised. If you were selecting this apartment because all utilities were included only to find out that you have to pay your electricity, that could be a deal breaker or a tool for negotiation. You should also get confirmation from your landlord if you need to set up a separate account for any utilities that they are covering or if everything will be covered under a master account.

At your lease signing you will be expected to provide first month's rent and your deposit. The deposit is usually equivalent to one-month's rent. This deposit will be used to cover any damages when you move out. If you care for your new place and are on good terms with your landlord your deposit will be returned to you -- when you move out. In some instances, landlords may request that you pay last month's rent up front. Meaning you will need to be prepared to pay three-months of rent just to move in. When you request the lease application you should get clarity of any moneys due at your lease signing.

If you are planning on moving to an apartment building you will need to get confirmation of their moving day rules. Buildings may require you to move during certain time of day and even on certain days. Typically during business hours in order not to inconvenience other tenants. Some building will even require you to schedule your moving day so that they can prep the building (lay down floor covers and hang elevator pads). More and more buildings are requiring Moving Day Deposits. This deposit is separate from your rent and security deposit. The moving day deposit will be returned to you upon the completion of your move and confirmation that nothing in building has been damaged by your move.

> **PRO TIP**
>
> If at all possible, coordinate your move date to be a few days before your first-time commitment. This will give you a chance to have a good night's rest before your first day of school or new job.

How to End a Lease

If for some reason things just do not work out for you in your new space, you have the right to end a lease. You will either have to give 30 or 60 days notice and in some cases you may be responsible for a fine. Details will be outlined in the lease agreement that you signed. In most case, if you break a lease early you will lose your deposit and you will not be able to use the landlord as a reference. So consider all options carefully before walking away.

FOLLOW THROUGH

Moving day is quickly approaching and it is time to pack your belongings, rent a van (if needed), and call utility companies to schedule turn-on services. There is more info on turn-on service in the following chapter. Since you are moving out for the first time you may not have much to pack beyond your clothes, toiletries, books, bedroom furniture and maybe a couch. But for some reason, packing always takes longer than you expect. And you never really understand how much stuff you have until you have to pack it.

Budgeting 3.0

Yep, another section on budgeting. This is a moving budget and it is separate from your monthly budget. This budget will help you account for all those miscellaneous line items that you incur on moving day.

While this budget will include the obvious like your first month's rent and security deposit, it also needs to include things like your moving day deposit, moving van, packing materials, and travel expenses (gas, hotel, tolls if needed). Below are a few line items that you should consider having some money allocated towards in a moving budget.

- First month's rent
- Last month's rent (if needed)
- Security deposit
- Move in deposit (if needed)
- Pet deposit (if needed)
- Pet sitting for the day (if needed)
- Spare key
- Moving van

- Movers (if needed)
- Moving supplies (boxes, tape, bubble wrap, moving paper, hand truck rental)
- Travel expenses (gas, hotel, tolls, airline tickets - if needed)
- Home improvement (allotting $50 for any miscellaneous items needed from a home improvement store would be wise)
- Plan to set aside some money to stock your pantry and fridge
- Cleaning supplies, toilet paper, paper towels, and a shower curtain
- Snacks for moving day
- Pizza & drinks for your family and friends who are helping

Packing

Moving is the perfect opportunity to take inventory of what you have and what you are going to take with you. So take the time to declutter and categorize all your stuff. As you are packing keep a box close by for donations and a bag for trash. Before you pack anything consider if this is something that you want in your new home and new life. Once you have your box of donation items, consider if anything is worth trying to sell on your own or worth taking it to a consignment store. A little extra cash to cover moving expenses feels awesome!

Be strategic about how you pack. Label all your boxes and bags, not just with a general label of the contents, but also what room it should go in e.g. bedroom/sheets. This will make unpacking less cumbersome.

There will be a few things that you will need to have readily available on moving day and the first few days of getting settled in your new space. I recommend packing these items separately and keeping them close by rather than loading them into the moving van.

Your suitcase can be packed like if you were going on vacation. It should include all your essentials:
- Clothes and shoes for first day 3-days of school/work
- Pajamas
- Toothbrush/toothpaste
- Face wash and body soap with wash rag
- Contact lenses/glasses supplies
- Deodorant
- Hygiene products: razor, shaving cream, hair brush and hair product, hair ties and nail polish remover

Other things that you should have easily accessible on moving day are:
- A shower curtain and hooks
- First aid kit
- Toilet paper
- Drinking water
- Snacks to keep you going
- Paper towels
- Cleaning supplies
- Pet food (if you have a pet)
- Kitchen cabinet liners

With this being your first move, there may be some apartment supplies that you do not have. Things like pots, pans, cooking utensils, and some furniture. Do not just assume that you have to buy everything new. While you may have to buy some stuff new, ask your parents if you can clean out some of their older kitchen supplies. Also consider going to a Goodwill or a second-hand store. These stores have some pretty cool "vintage" items that should be in good condition like a desk, dinner table and chairs, even a couch. Most Goodwill stores also have plate sets, coffee pots, toaster ovens, microwaves, etc. Just make sure that you wash and clean everything before you use it.

Before Moving In

All places will give you the opportunity to have a "walk through" of your new place. This is your chance to review the apartment empty and confirm what you are getting into. Walk throughs should be done during the day. Night time walk throughs are tricky because lighting can hide some pretty big imperfections. Take pictures and make note of any damages on the walls, scuffs on the floor, kitchen cabinets that do not work properly, and the state of the inside of the refrigerator and the oven. I also suggest testing the water pressure in all the faucets and drawing all the blinds to make sure that none are broken.

Once you have all this in place, send a reasonable list to the landlord or leasing office. This documentation is important because it relieves you of any blame or wrong-doing for those damages so you are not responsible for fixing them. The landlord may choose to fix some of the items or offer you a discount to your next month's rent if you decide to fix some of the minor items on your own. If you do need to fix it yourself, make sure that you get the landlord's confirmation that you will be reimburse once the work is completed.

At the walk through, you can ask the landlord if you can take the opportunity to bug bomb the apartment. You may not be able to do this if you are moving into a dorm or a shared space. You can purchase bug bombs from your local hardware store, relatively inexpensively. The reason for doing this in your apartment now is two-fold:

1) Your apartment is empty and there is nowhere for the bugs to hide.
2) You will not have anything to wash or clean after the fact to remove the chemicals from your sheets, glasses and silverware.

If you can get into the apartment the night before moving day that would be ideal. If not, I recommend doing it as soon as possible so that the chemicals have time to work before you have to clean it all out to start moving.

Moving Day

Before you start unloading boxes give your new place a good cleaning. Since it is empty it will make cleaning pretty easy and focused. This will be especially important if you are able to de-bug your new space. Clean the kitchen, bathrooms, and vacuum/sweep the floors.

On moving day your goal is to get all your stuff from point A to point B and return any rented equipment as soon as possible. Below are a few more pro tips to make moving day go smoothly.

PRO TIPS

Start your day with a healthy, protein packed breakfast that will keep you full for an extended period of time (donuts and coffee will have an ill-timed mid-move sugar crash).

Wear comfortable clothes and closed-toe shoes. You will be running around and carrying boxes; stylish jeans and flip flops are not ideal nor are they safe.

If you can rent a hand truck either from the hardware store or moving facility, this will help with moving multiple boxes at once.

Keep some cash on hand in case you need to tip; this will be helpful if you order take out for lunch or dinner.

Make sure everyone helping with the move has your old and new address and your phone number.

Pack a cooler with fruits, drinks and snacks, and if you are feeling up to it some sandwiches.

Keep your phone's ringer on loud and bring an extra charger or

> an external battery pack if you have one.
>
> Once you have cleaned the kitchen, set down cabinet liners, this is easiest to do when the kitchen is empty and will help with keeping your kitchen clean.
>
> Send someone to make a duplicate copy of your key.
>
> Connect your phone's hotspot to your laptop so that you have WIFI in the early days of the move.
>
> Check the weather forecast, moving in extreme cold, rain or snow could be dangerous.

Renter's Insurance

You may be thinking *"I don't have anything worth insuring"* but actually you do. Your computer, your camera, your PlayStation, your TV. These are all things that can be costly to replace if damaged or stolen. Renter's insurance is usually less than $20 per month and, in my opinion, totally worth it, especially if you are moving to a big city.

Something to consider, if there is a flood in your apartment and your stuff is damaged, your landlord's property insurance will NOT cover you. I speak from personal experience.

> ***True Story:*** *Spring 2006*
>
> I lived on the top floor of a 2-story house. We had had bad rain for three straight days. The gutters had not been cleared and the water on the roof had no way out. Eventually the roof collapsed into my room and onto my bed. My roommate's room had a door

> that lead to the roof. Water was rushing down those stairs into her room like it was Niagara Falls. Everything we owned was water damaged. Our clothes, beds, furniture, books, iPods, computers, and the TV. The landlord did not cover any of it.

Granted, this was worse case scenario. But piece of mind and knowing that you would at least have some help to replace your belongings may be worth your minimum monthly payment.

PRO TIP

> If you are interested in rental insurance coverage, call your car insurance company. They will be able to give you a quote that includes a multiple-coverage discount.

GETTING SETTLED

The hard part(s) are all over. Now it is just a matter of unpacking and getting settled in your new space and new city and all the little things that need to get sorted. Things may not feel like home yet, but once everything is away, boxes are gone, and you get into your routine, you will feel right at home.

Unpacking

Unpacking takes three times as long as packing and every time you move it takes longer. If you label your boxes as mentioned previously, it will make unpacking easier. Make sure the right boxes get into the right room. My advice to unpacking is take it one box at a time. Your initial goal is just to get rid of the boxes. You can take time to color coordinate your closet after all your clothes is put away.

You will need a place to sleep tonight, so you should sort out your bedroom first. Since you may have to rebuild furniture this will also likely take the most time and make the most noise. Putting away bathroom items is quiet enough to happen at any time. Conversely, your neighbors will not be too friendly if you are building furniture in the middle of the night.

Once your sleeping quarters are set up proceed to the kitchen and bathrooms. Your television and entertainment units should be last. If these are set up first it could be a distraction from what needs to be done.

PRO TIP

When you are all done packing, a lot of packing materials can be reused and recycled. Check in with a local off-site storage facility to see if they have a "take one, leave one" program. Or you can

> post them up on a community bulletin board for anyone preparing for an upcoming move.

Utilities

By now you should be very aware of what utilities are included with your rent and which you are responsible for. You should have called each of the utilities companies to schedule your service start date when you signed your lease. For some utilities like cable and internet, you will need to schedule a technician to come out and get you all hooked up.

> **PRO TIP**
>
> Do not schedule utility companies to come on moving day. Most times they need to know what your set up will be like so that they can get you the best coverage in your space. And having a technician underfoot on moving day will only add to the chaos of everything else that is happening.

You should keep a list of all your utilities companies, their contact information and your account numbers. This will come in handy if you ever have to call for service.

Address Change

You will need to get an address update packet from the post office. You can do this online at www.usps.com, but the online version requires a small fee for security purposes. The post office does everything that they can to make sure you get your mail but do not rely on them alone. Be proactive and contact your bank, student loan company, car loan lender, and credit cards directly to give them your new address.

Legal Documentation

In most states you have 30-days from the time you move to go to the DMV and get a new driver's license or ID. Try to make this a top priority so that you can coordinate your schedule. Local DMV website will tell you exactly what you need to bring with you to your appointment. The information requested varies from state to state, but make sure you bring everything with you so you do not have to make multiple trips. While you are at the DMV you can get your vehicle registered and surprise, surprise your voting registration sorted out. You do vote, don't you? This will save you time later in the year.

New Neighborhood

You should be feeling pretty good about your move at this point. Below are a few tips that I have curated to help you feel right at home in your new neighborhood.

PRO TIPS

> Explore your new neighborhood on foot! You would be amazed how many gems are hiding just around the corner.
>
> Pop into every restaurant and find out if they deliver and if they have take out menus, even if it is not food you are likely to eat. You can surprise and delight your guests with the variety of offerings.
>
> Go to the local grocery store and sign up for their customer rewards program.

Find the library and get a new card - you can rent more than just books - they have games, magazines, movies, music, audio books, digital copies of books, and WIFI -- ALL FOR FREE!

If you have a pet, find the closest pet clinic and get your pet registered. While you are at it, find the dog park, groomers, and pet suppliers.

Look through your contacts and see who, if anyone, lives close by. Reach out and ask them to give you a tour of the neighborhood.

Get to know your transportation options, you never know when you will need a lift. It would also make life a lot easier if you knew, beforehand, how to get to/from work or school on the bus, trolley, train, or subway. This is also a great way to explore your new area.

Pick up a copy of the local monthly and weekly papers or find the city activity calendar online. This will have information on events happening at the public spaces, parks and farmer's markets.

Update all your contacts. People move all the time. Take this opportunity to reach out to your contacts to get their most up-to-date, address, phone number and email address.

Find the closest laundromat and dry cleaners - regardless if you plan to use it or not.

Put up curtains around big windows, this will help keeping cooling and heating costs down.

Check with your local utilities companies' website, most feature creative ways to reduce your monthly usage.

Visit your local farmer's markets. They have more than just onions! They have locally made and grown goods and services like desserts, pastries, meats, dairy, veggies, and fruits. Some even have community composting, music and street performers.

Log onto community websites like www.nextdoor.com. The will keep you informed of upcoming events or even crime in your area.

Visit the local parks. Most host free seasonal community events. You can also use the park as your personal gym.

Talk to your neighbors. You may find a new friend or something to do.
Organize your space. Decorate, but ask before painting. Most landlords don't mind but may ask you to paint it back to white before you hand over the keys.

Become your own best friend. Take yourself on a date! Go to a solo dinner and see a movie.

The majority of laundromats offer drop off service that do your laundry and fold it for a price by the pound that is comparable to doing it yourself. If you've had a busy month -- let someone else do the laundry while you rest up.

CONCLUSION

Congratulations! You are now living on your own. You should feel proud of yourself for getting through what is usually a stressful situation. Moving is one of those things in life that you do over and over again and while it may get easier, it is never easy. As long as you do your due diligence and do not rush into anything you should be able to save yourself from Buyer's Remorse or an expensive mistake.

Remember, when you are renting you are borrowing someone else's space, and they expect you to take care of it as if it were your own. Be respectful both of your new "borrowed" home, your roommates and your housemates and you will have a great experience.

Now GET LOST! No really, go and explore your new neighborhood. If you get too lost, just ask Siri to get you back home.

APPENDIX

A. Setting Expectations

B. Apartment Hunting Checklist

C. Sample Residential Lease Agreement

AMENITIES WANTED

KEY QUESTIONS

Is there anything in my life that I just cannot live without?

What will a typical day be like for me?

Should I take my family pet with me or leave them home?

MUST-HAVE   # NICE-TO-HAVE

APARTMENT CHECKLIST

Address

Rent Price

Size (Sqft)

Beds / Baths

Unit Condition

Washer / Dryer

Outdoor Space

Windows / View

Heating & Cooling

Utilities Included

Parking

Building Condition

Smoke Detectors

Building Security

Nearest School

Nearest Grocery

Nearest Library

Public Transit Access

Nearest Friend / Family

Notes

Town / Region

Unit / Floor #   Elevator | Stairs

Available Date

Deposits

Rent Duration

Pets Allowed

Street Noise

Kitchen / Appliances

Commons / Garden

Swimming Pool

Furniture

Blinds / Curtains

Area Walkability

Nearest Bank

Nearest Religious Fac.

Nearest Gym

Nearest Theater

Cafes / Restaurants

SAMPLE LEASE AGREEMENT   RESIDENTIAL

The Premises are offered without regard to race, color, religion, gender, national origin, ancestry, physical disability or handicap, or any other class or category of protection.

This Agreement is entered into this _____ day of _____, 20____, by and between _____ (collectively, referred to as "Owner") and _____, (referred to as "Lessee", whether one or more individuals).

1. **CONTRACTED PREMISES**: The parties agree that Lessee shall rent from Owner the property located at _____ in _____, _____ _____, (hereinafter "Premises") to be used and occupied only by Lessee as a residence for Lessee, and for no other purposes, for the term of this contract.

2. **CONTRACT**: This contract shall begin _____ and end _____. It is expressly understood that this lease is for the entire term set forth above, and the fact that Lessee should no longer be a resident of the community in which the Premises are located, should be transferred, should cease to be actively enrolled in a college in this community, or for any other reason be unable to continue in the unit, Lessee's responsibility shall nonetheless continue for the full term hereof. Lessee understands and acknowledges that Owner would suffer damages if this lease is breached prior to the expiration of its term, including cleanup cost, re-rental commissions, and advertising costs. Therefore, the parties agree that if this lease is breached prior to the expiration date, Owner shall be entitled to retain the security deposit as liquidated damages. However, Lessee's liability is not limited to the amount of the security deposit, but includes and is not limited to, all unpaid installments of the lease and damages to the Premises, in excess of the security

deposit.

3. **RENT**. The total rent for the Premises shall be the sum of $_____ each month ($_____ term total), with payment to be made by Lessee to Owner, without demand, on the first day of each month. Lessee shall pay a $30.00 late fee on unpaid balances received after the 1st of the month, with an additional $5.00 accrued for each day payment is late thereafter (for example, a payment made on the 4th would include a $40.00 late fee). All payments shall be made to Owner at _____. In the event of insufficient funds, an additional fee of $30.00, plus all applicable late fees, shall apply. A 10% carry-over fee shall be charged on all outstanding balances not paid on or before the last day of each month. If Lessee is more than one individual, each individual Lessee shall be jointly and severally liable for the total rent due, including any fees, regardless of whether Lessee typically pays the rent in collective or individual payments.

4. **SECURITY DEPOSIT**: Upon execution of this lease, Owner acknowledges receipt from Lessee of a security deposit equal to one month's rent ($_____.00), which shall be held by Owner as security against loss from damage; nonpayment of rent; or any other breach of this lease or the _____ Residential Landlord/Tenant Act, K.S.A. 58-2540 et seq.; by Lessee. The security deposit shall be refunded to Lessee(s) who made such payment within thirty (30) days after the expiration of this lease, less any damages for nonpayment of rent, breach of this lease or the Landlord/Tenant Act, or damage to the Premises. Lessee must follow proper checkout procedures and agrees to provide Owner with forwarding address in writing. The security deposit is not any part of the rent herein reserved and consequently cannot be applied to the final month's rent. This security deposit shall be held without any duty to pay interest and shall be held in accordance with the Landlord/Tenant Act.

5. **PETS/PET DEPOSIT**: Lessee shall not keep or allow on the Premises any pet or other animal without Owner's prior written approval. If Owner permits a pet or animal to be kept on the Premises (one pet maximum), Lessee shall pay a pet security deposit equal to one-half of one-month's rent. Lessee shall pay an additional $50/month in rent for said pet or animal, pursuant to the terms Paragraph 3. In no

case shall Lessee keep or allow on the Premises, or ask Owner to keep or allow on the Premises, any animal that is not permitted within the State of _____, _____ County, or City of _____, or any dog that has been determined to be dangerous by a governmental entity.

6. **SEVERALTY**: In the event the Premises are rented to more than one individual, each of them shall be JOINTLY AND SEVERALLY LIABLE for the performance of the terms and conditions of this lease. Each individual Lessee understands and acknowledges that there is joint and several responsibility with respect to the total leased Premises and, accordingly, must exercise responsibility to see that the entire unit is used in compliance with this Agreement.

7. **UTILITIES & MAINTENANCE**: Lessee shall maintain the following utilities at the Premises: electricity and/or gas, water and sewer service, and trash. Lessee shall pay for all utilities required by this Agreement or desired by Lessee. Utilities shall be in a Lessee's name on the date lease begins and remain in a Lessee's name until lease expiration. Lessee shall provide Owner with confirmation numbers for each utility account. Lessee shall be responsible for removing Lessee's name from any utility accounts upon lease expiration.

Electric: _____

Water: _____

Trash: _____

8. **CARE OF THE PREMISES**: Lessee accepts the Premises in the present condition. It is the Lessee's responsibility at the time of moving in to provide Owner with a list of defects related to the Premises. Lessee agrees to keep and maintain the Premises in good clean condition, and to make no alterations or additions thereon or therein without the prior written consent of Owner. The Lessee will pay for misuse to plumbing, windows, doors, walls, cabinets, flooring, or any other aspect of the Premises and repay Owner for the cost of all repairs made necessary by neglect and careless use of the Premises. Owner shall invoice Lessee for any charges,

including a reasonable charge for management overhead, for labor and replacement costs of any damaged items other than normal wear and tear. Lessee shall immediately report to Owner and local police authority any criminal act causing damage to the Premises. Lessee agrees to promptly report any repairs that need to be made to the Premises to Owner. No Lessee incurred expense shall be deducted from the monthly rent under any circumstances whatsoever. Lessee agrees to do the following: keep the leased Premises, the grounds, common hallways and parking lots as clean and safe as their condition permits;

a. Remove from the Premises and grounds all rubbish, garbage, animal droppings, and other waste in a clean and safe manner;

b. Use all electrical, plumbing, appliances, sanitary, heating and air conditioning and fixtures in a safe and reasonable manner;

c. Be responsible for any destruction, defacement, damage, impairment, or removal of any part of the Premises caused by an act or omission of the Lessee or by any person or animal on the Premises at any time with the expressed or implied consent of Lessee;

d. Not engage in conduct, or allow any person or animal on the Premises with expressed or implied permission to engage in conduct, that will disturb the quiet and peaceful enjoyment of the Premises of other Tenants;

e. Obey all laws of the United States, the State of _____, and the ordinances of the City of _____, _____. In the event the Lessee or any invitee of the Lessee is convicted or diverted for a criminal offense occurring in or around the Premises, Owner shall have the right to terminate this lease immediately. Violation of this paragraph shall not only be a breach of the lease, but, in addition, Lessee agrees to reimburse Owner for any damages Owner suffers by reason of such violations;

f. Maintain the thermostat at a minimum of 55 degrees Fahrenheit when outdoor temperature will drop to freezing or below;

g. Not smoke, or allow any other person to smoke, inside the Premises at any time;

h. Change the furnace filter every 3 months or more frequently;

i. Replace batteries in smoke detectors as needed, and Lessee shall not remove smoke detectors or batteries from smoke detectors;

j.	Remove plumbing clogs from sink drains, tub drains, and toilets. Both the owner and tenant mutually agree that all toilets and drains are in working order unless Lessee notifies Owner otherwise, in writing, on the move-in day;

k.	Disconnect hoses or other attachments from outside water faucets, when outdoor temperature may drop to freezing or below.

l.	Pay a $25 fee to Owner if they lose their copy of the lease and request an additional copy.

m.	Purchase and change light bulbs in their apartment & immediately outside their door in common hallways within their building.

9.	**SUBLEASING**: Lessee shall not sublease without the prior written approval of Owner. If subleasing is approved, Lessee shall remain responsible for payment of rent and utilities until expiration of this lease. A one-time, $100.00 sublet fee must be paid prior to the subleaser occupying the Premises.

10.	**LEASE TERMINATION**: This lease shall automatically terminate at the end of the term identified herein. Should Lessee wish to sign a new lease for another year, Lessee shall notify Owner of such intention to sign a new lease by January 20, 20 . Lessee understands that this lease expires at 12:00 P.M. noon on the last day of the lease. In the absence of a new lease, Lessee shall vacate the Premises by the termination date and time without further notice from Owner. Any unauthorized holdover by Lessee shall be deemed a month-to-month tenancy. The holdover Lessee shall be liable to the Owner for 1½ months rent or 1½ times the actual damages suffered by Owner, whichever is greater.

11.	**NONLIABILITY OF OWNER & RENTER'S INSURANCE**: Except to the extent caused by Owner's willful negligence, Owner shall not be liable for damages, injury to persons, or loss of property of Lessee, and Lessee's invitees and guests, caused by any act or omission including but not limited to criminal act, fire, water, rain, acts of God, interruption of utilities and such similar reasons. Lessee shall hold Owner harmless for any such damage, injury, or loss. Lessee agrees that Lessee has been advised by Owner to secure renter's insurance from the above and other similar losses, including personal liability.

12. **RIGHT OF ENTRY & INSPECTION**: Owner reserves the right at all times to enter the Premises in case of emergency. Owner reserves the right at all reasonable times, and upon reasonable notice (either orally or written), to enter the Premises to make inspections, repairs, improvements; to supply necessary or requested services; to show the Premises to prospective or actual purchasers, tenants, workmen, or contractors; or to correct any breach of the lease or Rules and Regulations. If an inspection is required by a governmental agency, Lessee shall allow the governmental officials to enter the Premises to make such inspection. If Lessee notifies Owner of necessary repairs, Owner shall have the right to enter the Premises at any time for the purpose of making such repairs without further notification to Lessee. Lessee cannot change or add locks without prior written permission from Owner.

13. **DEFAULT**: If Lessee defaults in the payment of rent, abandons the Premises, or violates any other term of this lease, Owner may take any action permitted in law or equity, including declaring this lease terminated, and may elect to relet the Premises, charging Lessee for any deficiencies and costs related thereto. Lessee's absence from the Premises for seven (7) consecutive days while any portion of rent is delinquent shall give Owner the right to declare the Premises abandoned. Upon any violation herein, Owner shall have the right to institute a forcible entry and detainer action in the proper Court, obtain a writ of restitution and pursue all other remedies allowed by law.

14. **CARPET CLEANING**: Lessee shall have carpets professionally cleaned prior to move out, after all personal belongings have been removed. Lessee shall provide to Owner written proof showing the date on which the carpets were cleaned by a professional carpet cleaning company. If Lessee fails to have carpets professionally cleaned, fails to provide written proof of such, or if the carpets are cleaned unsatisfactorily, Owner may professionally clean or replace the carpets upon the Lessee's vacating the Premises and charge the Lessee accordingly. Steam cleaning of the carpets with a Rug Doctor or similar machine is not acceptable.

15.   **PESTS AND INFESTATIONS**: Lessee acknowledges that the Premises are free from all pests and infestations. Lessee shall maintain the Premises in this manner. In the event that extermination for any type of pest or infestation becomes necessary, the costs thereof will be assessed to Lessee for their units and any spread thereof to adjoining units. Routine spraying for spiders, ants, and other common bugs will be the responsibility of the lessee.

16.   **NOTIFICATION TO OWNER**: Lessee shall notify Owner of any absence from the Premises for more than seven (7) days. The Lessee shall notify Owner or Owner's agent promptly of any damage to the Premises or common areas caused by Lessee or Lessee's invitees, family, or animals, or any other damage of which Lessee has knowledge.

17.   **MOVE OUT**: It is the responsibility of Lessee to schedule a move-out inspection with Owner prior to moving out. Lessees must all be present for the move-out inspection. All Lessees' belongings shall be removed from the Premises and all carpet cleaning shall be completed prior to the move out inspection. If the Premises are NOT ready to be inspected at the time of the scheduled appointment (all furniture removed, all keys returned and unit cleaned and empty) a $50.00 re-inspection fee will be assessed to each Lessee.

18.   **ABANDONED PROPERTY**: Any personal property of Lessee remaining on the Premises, in any storage space, or otherwise in or about the building of which the Premises are a part, after the termination hereof, shall be deemed to be abandoned by Lessee, and Owner may remove, keep and/or dispose of such property, at Owner's discretion, without any liability to Owner. If Owner disposes of abandoned property, Lessee shall pay the costs therefor by deduction from the security deposit or reimbursement to Owner.

19.   **RULES AND REGULATIONS**: Lessee shall comply with and be bound by the Rules and Regulations attached hereto as "Exhibit A" and incorporated herein by reference. The Rules and Regulations shall be considered terms and conditions of this Lease, and any violation thereof shall be considered a breach of this Lease.

Owner may modify and amend the Rules and Regulations, at Owner's sole discretion. Provided that, any amendment shall not take effect until after fourteen (14) days written notice has been given to Lessee.

20. **LEAD-BASED PAINT**: Housing built before 1978 may contain lead-based paint. Lead from paint, paint chips, and dust can pose health hazards if not managed properly. Lead exposure is especially harmful to young children and pregnant women. Before renting pre-1978 housing, Owner must disclose the presence of known lead-based paint and/or lead-based paint hazards in the dwelling. Lessees must also receive a federally approved pamphlet on lead poisoning prevention. Owner has no knowledge of lead-based paint and/or lead-based paint hazards in the housing. Owner has no reports or records pertaining to lead-based paint and/or lead-based paint hazards in the housing. By signing this lease, Lessee acknowledges that Lessee has received copies of all information listed above and the pamphlet Protect Your Family From Lead in Your Home.

21. **SEVERABILITY & ENTIRE AGREEMENT**: This lease is subject to the Landlord/Tenant Act and its provisions should be construed in the light of that Act, except as modified herein. In the event any provision of this lease shall be held invalid, such provision shall be deemed severed from this lease without affecting the validity of the remaining provisions. This lease shall be binding on the heirs, administrators, executors and assigns of the parties and constitutes the entire agreement between the parties. No oral agreements or representations shall be binding on either party.

22. **ASSIGNMENT OF LEASE**: Owner reserves the right to assign the lease, should ownership change.

23. **ACKNOWLEDGMENT**: THIS IS A LEGALLY BINDING CONTRACT. DO NOT SIGN THIS DOCUMENT UNLESS YOU HAVE READ IT AND UNDERSTAND IT. LESSEE HEREBY ACKNOWLEDGES HAVING READ THIS LEASE AND THE RULES AND REGULATIONS. LESSEE AFFIRMS THAT LESSEE WILL, IN ALL RESPECTS, COMPLY WITH THE TERMS AND PROVISIONS OF THIS LEASE.

LESSEE ACKNOWLEDGES THAT THIS LEASE IS LEGALLY ENFORCEABLE AGAINST LESSEE AND ANY GUARANTOR IN ACCORDANCE WITH ITS TERMS AND CONDITIONS. THIS LEASE CONTAINS ALL AGREEMENTS BETWEEN THE PARTIES HEREIN AND ANY AGREEMENTS NOT CONTAINED HEREIN SHALL NOT BE BINDING. LESSEE ACKNOWLEDGES RECEIPT OF A COPY OF THIS LEASE.

IN WITNESS HEREOF, the parties have executed this lease on this, the _____ day of _____, 20____.

Owner/Agent's Signature: _____ Print Name: _____

Lessee's Signature: _____ Print Name: _____

Lessee's Signature: _____ Print Name: _____

About the Author

Elizabeth Peek has been obsessed with real estate from a young age. Her mother would take her to open houses on the weekends; and by the time she was 10, she would ride along with her aunt while she toured her properties, collected rents, and inspected construction sites for homes that she was remodeling.

Elizabeth received a Master of Science in Communications at the University of Florida and pursued a career in advertising in New York City. After a decade she made moving people around NYC her full time business as a rental and sales Realtor. In 2015 she moved to Kansas with her husband and newborn son and continued her work in Real Estate, personal investment properties, and managing renters of her own.

www.ingramcontent.com/pod-product-compliance
Lightning Source LLC
Chambersburg PA
CBHW051334220526
45468CB00004B/1635